# Nothing Is Ever One Thing

*Flash & Micro Fiction*

## Robert Scotellaro

BLUE LIGHT PRESS ◆ 1ST WORLD PUBLISHING

1st WORLD
PUBLISHING

SAN FRANCISCO ◆ FAIRFIELD ◆ DELHI

*Nothing Is Ever One Thing*

1ST WORLD LIBRARY
106 South Court Street
Fairfield, Iowa 52556
www.1stworldpublishing.com

BLUE LIGHT PRESS
www.bluelightpress.com
Email: bluelightpress@aol.com

BOOK & COVER DESIGN
Melanie Gendron
melaniegendron999@gmail.com

COVER ART
*Steampunk – Gears – Inner Workings* by Mike Savad
http://mikesavad.com
With permission granted

AUTHOR PHOTO
Diana Scott

FIRST EDITION

Library of Congress Cataloging-in-Publication Data

ISBN 978-1-4218-3633-1

# ALSO BY ROBERT SCOTELLARO

## Anthology

*NEW MICRO*:
*Exceptionally Short Fiction*
Co-edited with James Thomas

## Fiction

*Bad Motel*
*What We Know So Far*
*Measuring the Distance*

## Poetry

*After the Revolution*
*The Night Sings A Capella*
*Rhapsody of Fallen Objects*
*My Father's Cadillac*
*Early Love Poems of Genghis Khan*
*Blinded by Halos*
*East Harlem Poems*

## For Children

*Snail Stampede*
*Dancing with Frankenstein*
*Carla and the Greedy Merchant*
*The Terrible Storm*

# ACKNOWLEDGEMENTS

Grateful acknowledgement is made to the following publications in which these stories or earlier versions previously appeared:

*Flash*: *The International Short-Short Story Magazine*:
    "Smoke Signals," "Sewn In," "Stuffed,"
    "Some Like It Hot," "The Magician's Lover," "Gigolo
    in Late Bloom (In Triptych)," "Dragonfly in Lieu of a
    Chopper," "Stuntman in Still Life"
*The Journal of Compressed Creative Arts*: "so much depends…"
*100 Word Story*: "Erasure," "A Change of Clothes"
*Nothing Short of 100 (Selected Tales from 100 Word Story)*:
    "A Change of Clothes"
*Microfiction Monday/Microfiction Monday's 2015 Anthology*:
    "The Small End of the Funnel"
*Connotation Press*: "Straight to It," "Transplant,"
    "The Widow on Fire (A Micro-Fable)"
*Bending Genres Journal*: "Nothing Is Ever One Thing"
*Meniscus Literary Journal*: "A Neighbor in the Rain"
*Dogzplot*: "Sonic Boom"
*Flash Frontier*: "The Metamorphosis Revisited (A Micro-Fable)"
*Spelk*: "Voice-overs"
*Pure Slush ENVY (7 Deadly Sins Vol. 6)*:
    "Brief Encounter with Giant Hamburger in the Snow"
*Right Hand Pointing*: "Gun with a Conscience (A Micro-Fable)"
*Vine Leaves Literary Journal/The Best of Vine Leaves Literary*
    *Journal 2012*: "Skyped"
*Flash Boulevard*: "The Weight of Certain Moments,"
    "The Fall and Rise of Milton Brent," "Side Effects,"
    "The King of Non Sequiturs," "Talking Dummies,"
    "All the Seasons We Have Never Known," "A Thing
    with Feathers," "Interrogating the Dead," "Little Heads"

*River of Earth and Sky Anthology*:
    "A Horse with a Fork in Its Head (A Micro-Fable)"
*Willows Wept Review*: "Pretty Rain (A Micro-Fable)"
*Bad Motel*: "Smoke Signals," "The Small End of the Funnel,"
    "Sonic Boom," "Sewn In," "Erasure," "Ballet, Sinus
    Headaches, and a Decent Steak"
*Six Sentences*: "High Fidelity"
*Tuesday Shorts/Tuesday Shorts Anthology*: "High Fidelity"
*Postcard Shorts*: "The Grudge Farmer (A Micro-Fable)"
*Fictive Dream*: "Mr. Wizard"
*Flash Fiction Magazine*: "Oxalis"
*Rhapsody of Fallen Objects*: "Athletic Secrets (A Public
    Service Announcement)"
*Madroad: The Breadline Press West Coast Anthology:*
    "The Mountain That Spit up Pianos (A Micro-Fable),"
    "A Horse with a Fork in its Head (A Micro-Fable)"
*The Night Sings A Capella*: "The Mountain That Spit Up Pianos
    (A Micro-Fable)"
*Eclectic Flash Magazine*: "The Limits of Art (A Micro-Fable)"
*Measuring the Distance*: "The Limits of Art (A Micro- Fable),"
    "Saw Blade," "Stuffed," "Stick," "Freeway Jesus"
*Postcard Shorts*: "The Sin Suit (A Micro-Fable)"
*Pure Slush Vol. 15*: "Geisha"
*The Linnet's Wings*: "Rhapsody of Fallen Objects (A Public
    Service Reminder)"
*Rhapsody of Fallen Objects*: "Rhapsody of Fallen Objects (A
    Public Service Reminder"
*Postcard Poems and Prose Magazine*: "Ballet, Sinus Headaches,
    And a Decent Steak"
*White Knuckle Press*: "A Horse with a Fork in Its Head
    (A Micro-Fable)"
*What We Know So Far*: "Some Like It Hot," "so much depends…"
*Long Story Short*: " Hawaiian Shirt"
*Sleep Is a Beautiful Colour (National Flash-Fiction Day
    2017 Anthology)*: "A Sky Full of Ghosts"

*for Diana*

*"The web of our life is of a mingled yarn, good and ill together..."*

—William Shakespeare

# CONTENTS

A Neighbor in the Rain ........................................................ 13

Brief Encounter with a Giant Hamburger in the Snow ...... 15

Nothing Is Ever One Thing ................................................ 16

The Weight of Certain Moments ........................................ 19

The Fall and Rise of Milton Brent ..................................... 20

Superwoman at the Edge ................................................... 21

The Magician's Lover ......................................................... 24

Pretty Rain (A Micro-Fable) .............................................. 25

so much depends... ............................................................ 26

Smoke Signals .................................................................... 27

High Fidelity ...................................................................... 28

The Grudge Farmer (A Micro-Fable) ................................. 29

Mr. Wizard ........................................................................ 30

The Small End of the Funnel ............................................. 32

Oxalis ................................................................................ 33

Late Blooming Gigolo (In Triptych) .................................. 35

Athletic Secrets (A Public Service Announcement) ........... 36

The Mountain That Spit Up Pianos (A Micro-Fable) ........ 37

A Visit to the Nervous Hospital ......................................... 38

Dragonfly in Lieu of a Chopper ......................................... 39

A Piece of Sky .................................................................... 40

The Limits of Art (A Micro-Fable) ..................................... 41

The Need to Know ............................................................. 42

Stuntman in Still Life ........................................................ 43

Sonic Boom ....................................................................... 44

Whiteout ............................................................................ 45

Sewn In .............................................................................. 46

Erasure ............................................................................... 47

The Sin Suit (A Micro-Fable) ............................................ 48

Ketchup ............................................................................. 49

Voice-overs ........................................................................ 50

Straight to It .................................................................. 52
Geisha ........................................................................... 53
Saw Blade ..................................................................... 54
A Change of Clothes ...................................................... 55
Rhapsody of Fallen Objects (A Public Service Reminder) .. 56
A Different Song ............................................................ 57
A Thing with Feathers .................................................... 58
The Viking and the Elephant Trainer's Great-Great Grandson . 59
Stuffed .......................................................................... 61
Gun with a Conscience (A Micro-Fable) ......................... 63
Side Effects ................................................................... 64
Strangers in a Strange Land ........................................... 66
Skyped .......................................................................... 68
Time Machine ............................................................... 69
The King of Non Sequiturs ............................................ 70
The Metamorphosis Revisited ........................................ 72
Ballet, Sinus Headaches, and a Decent Steak .................. 73
The Mermaid and the Laughing Santa ............................ 74
A Horse with a Fork in Its Head (A Micro-Fable) ............ 75
Talking Dummies .......................................................... 76
The Old Woman and Her Breezy Blue Islands ................. 77
Stick ............................................................................. 79
Transplant ..................................................................... 80
The Widow on Fire (A Micro-Fable) ............................... 81
Little Heads ................................................................... 82
Freeway Jesus ................................................................ 83
Some Like It Hot ........................................................... 85
The Incredible Shrinking Woman ................................... 86
Hawaiian Shirt .............................................................. 87
A Sky Full of Ghosts ..................................................... 89
Interrogating the Dead ................................................... 91
In the City of Fog and Mist (A Micro-Fable) .................. 92
All the Seasons We Have Never Known .......................... 93

About the Author .......................................................... 95

# A Neighbor in the Rain

She was standing in the rain in a gray bikini. It was coming down hard. The bathing suit was modest by bikini standards, and she wore it like Mona Lisa wore a smile. I could see her from my deck. Earlier she had slathered herself with sunscreen and lay on a blanket with her nose deep in a paperback. Now the book was mush, the blanket soaked, and she didn't seem to mind. I was under an overhang so I was dry and enjoying the music the rain was making against the corrugated plastic.

She looked up at the heavens through the pelting downpour. A cat came to the edge of her sliding door, sniffed the air, then ran back in as if chased. Our kids went to the same school but were in different grades so never played together. Her husband was an airline pilot and was rarely home. He liked to travel, she told me once. "I've got the kids," she said. It was a solemn declaration.

She looked up at the sky and I thought she might curse it, but she opened her mouth and welcomed in the rain. Held her arms out, palms up, taking it all in. I wondered if she hated what she was reading, baked and sweaty. If the characters were in some exotic land, madly in love or trapped in a foreign prison, or just the usual suspects trying to get by–feeling the carousel breeze on a hot day–if one stood close enough–the world spinning. These summer storms were rare and perhaps this was an unexpected adventure. An oasis that suddenly appeared. There was all that sand.

One of her children came to the door and called out, "*Mom!*" and the trance was broken. A black lab ran out into the rain and beat its tail against her leg until she lowered her arms to pet it. She gathered up the soggy blanket and book, and I hoped she'd turn and wave. But she didn't and went inside instead with the dog in tow.

I picked up my own book from my lap. But somehow the words that had sparked moments earlier, seemed dull and plodding.

Moments come and go. And clocks do not always tell the truth, and moments have their own sense of time, and that one did not last nearly long enough. The rain too was short-lived. The way summer storms often are.

My own child called out from two rooms away to tell me to "Come quick!"—that Baxter was drinking from the toilet bowl again. I pulled a leaf from a potted plant and used it for a bookmark. I closed the novel and gave it a chance to recharge. Was sure it would read better when I'd find the time to get back to it, with an empty head again.

# Brief Encounter with a Giant Hamburger in the Snow

He told her he wanted a life that was more like ejecting from a jet plane than getting up from a saggy couch. But he ran out of jets and now the latter prevailed. He was wearing a giant hamburger suit, and said inside it beat the heart of a poet. They stood outside a chain restaurant and smoked cigarettes. It had started to snow and he told her how he once serenaded a girlfriend in fifteen-degree weather, standing under her window with a boom box held over his head.

He told her how he'd like to open up a junkyard someday. "Rusty gold," he said. He told her sometimes he read the Periodic Table of the Elements aloud, just to hear the elegant sounds of those words. He told her how the ancient Egyptians used to think bats had perfect eyesight because of the bugs they snatched out of the air. That they believed a drop of bat's blood in each eye could cure blindness.

He said, "So much for assumptions." That he wasn't going to be a giant hamburger or hotdog forever. Said he envied those who glided through life without a care. He said, "Hey, give me your number and maybe we could, you know…"

She said, "Sure," and wrote some numbers she made up on the back of one of the flyers he was handing out.

"Okay," she said.

"Okay," he said.

Then, "Damn," under his breath as he watched her cross the street and vanish into a crowd. "She's really something."

Gathering snowflakes landed on the rubber ketchup, lettuce, and tomatoes surrounding him, and he didn't mind the cold or the wind one bit. It was a beautiful day.

# Nothing Is Ever One Thing

The plane crashed into the mountain. It had lost altitude suddenly, irredeemably. There was chaos in the cockpit. Seatbelts clicked shut, oxygen masks dropped. Then a monstrous fiery blast...

• • •

Roger, speaking in gasps after running through the airport, deposited that red face of his over the boarding counter and complained fecklessly. How the hell did he know it would take so long... Those ridiculously long lines...

"I'm sorry," the boarding agent said, peering into all that fury. "That flight has taken off some time ago. You'll need to rebook."

"*Fuck!*" he said, slapping his hand down hard on the counter, and a security guard rushed forward.

• • •

Roger rocketed through traffic. Till he couldn't. There was a foundation makeup convention he desperately needed to be at. There was a promotion waiting to fatten his wallet if he got it right. This new product he'd pitch. This new old product with a fresh new name and ad campaign he'd pitch. The clients he needed to get onboard would be there, and he knew the script by heart. But there was a plane to catch between him and success, and now he was the one, *goddammit*, who needed to get onboard. Just his luck that there was more traffic than he expected, and that friggin' gold fish. *What was he thinking?*

• • •

He was scrambling out of the bedroom with his suitcase when he saw his young daughter in the hall crying. *Now what?* he thought, looking at his watch. She had a small fishbowl in her hands with a goldfish floating on the top of the water, her tears dripping into it.

"14 Karat," she said, then sobbed. His wife was already downstairs, naked under her robe, fixing lunch for their eldest to take to school.

"I'm so sorry, hon," he said, patting her head. "Let's flush 14 Karat down the toilet together, so it can go in the ocean. Be in the big water where it belongs."

She hugged the bowl against herself tightly. "No!" she screeched. "He'll go to hell then!"

"Hell?"

She released one hand and pointed down at the carpet. "I want him to go to heaven," she said. "We have to bury him like Grandpa, for him to go to heaven."

For God's sake, he thought, but went with her out back and buried it under the honeysuckle. There was a little girl ritual and a little girl prayer in whispers as he bowed his head and glanced furtively at his watch.

$\bullet\ \bullet\ \bullet$

While slipping on his trousers he looked out the window. After three days of incessant downpours, it had finally let up. He stood there sunlit. The storm had moved on. Perhaps that meant something, the storm moving on. Clear skies. That maybe he'd get some kind of break. He went over some pitch lines in front of the mirror. Maybe longer than he had time for. But so much was riding on it. When he felt he was ready, he grabbed his suitcase/the doorknob. Then he heard it from the other side of the door. Thought *What the hell...?*

$\bullet\ \bullet\ \bullet$

The alarm clock startled him awake. His wife stirred. He pulled back the comforter and gazed at the teepee his erection made of his boxers. He didn't want to cut it close. But there

17

was still time. A quickie wouldn't change much. And besides, he needed to rid himself of some of that tension that was building. He strapped on his watch without looking at it, reached over, with a pestering hand, into all that warmth…

# The Weight of Certain Moments

The bank guard went down like a sack of lead fishing weights. Then the gun swung toward Gwen, along with those frenzied eyes, then everyone else, and finally, the teller.

He said: "Don't fucking move!" And they froze. The teller kept filling the bag with cash. He waved his gun around again at the statues they'd become, then bolted for the door. Gwen watched the red-ugly spread as the guard groaned.

After the detectives were done, she stood at the bus stop and thought of her young daughter singing a chicken song earlier, how silly, precious the moment was. She noticed the way a couple's words, in the chilled air, turned to vanishing smoke as they frosted back and forth.

When the bus came it was dark out, and in the yellow window light she saw someone gazing blankly out as if nothing had happened, as if her heart was not still racing. Thought how odd that was. How what is known and what is not can co-exist so closely in ignorance. Later she/they'd watch it all on the news.

It was not her bus. She stood there and waited for the next one. From the noisy exhaust, as the bus left, a few dead leaves flew up, behaving like butterflies for an instant. And she, despite herself, thought, how lovely.

# The Fall and Rise of Milton Brent

Maybe it goes like this: A man works in a rake factory. He punches a clock, catches the same bus home, the same time, eats alone. A life about as uniform, as interesting, as a bowl haircut. Maybe one day the stars align just so, or the earth tilts a bit, this way or that. More likely it is none of these things. So when he passes that building on fire, and the woman out the window, three stories up, screams down at him, through the smoke, less than a minute or two before the fire trucks arrive with their long ladders, and he raises his head in time to see the baby she will drop through that seemingly endless channel of air into his hands like a high fly ball fallen from the heavens, into those able rake-stacking hands, his TV-dinner-eating beefy fingers. A synchronicity nearly balletic in its grace. The baby screaming, the trucks' screaming arrival. The eager fireman that takes it: the blanket, the oxygen, the ladders telescoping up. Onlookers cheering. The whole thing from iPhones to YouTube–viral. The Rake Man's promotion finally coming through, the Firemen's Hero Award on stage. The news anchors showing it all in slo-mo, again and again... The new microwave ticking off the TV dinner's heat for two now. The rakes in yards piling up the leaves of strangers, leaning against fences afterwards. A fire somewhere else. Good luck/bad luck. Some dry leaves racing down the street, some other street, like they had somewhere important to go.

# Superwoman at the Edge

She was standing on the other side of the protective railing at the edge of the Grand Canyon, gazing into that scenic abyss. I didn't want to startle her, and I didn't want her to make a play at being Superwoman either.

"Great view," I said. She turned, and a few loose stones fell over the side.

"It's so empty," she said.

"Empty?"

"Yeah, good empty. Everything is so filled in. But not this place."

I was hoping she wasn't planning to change that in some small way. "Don't you think it would be safer on the other side of that railing?"

"Oh, sure," she said. "If that's what you're looking for. Wanna join me?"

"No, I'm good." She laughed. It was chopped, mirthless.

"I bet you think I'm going to jump."

"I didn't say that."

"Sure you did. It's in your voice. It doesn't take a genius to figure that out. Bet you've gone your whole life thinking you're so clever at disguising what you really mean."

"How would you know?"

"That's more like it."

"Quit acting so superior," I told her, losing sight of the situation.

"That's a long way down," she said, reminding me.

"Come on, quit it." I held out my hand and walked a bit closer.

"Don't," she said. I stopped, stood there. She turned back.

"What's so great about this life anyway?" she said.

"You're young and beautiful," I heard myself say, wishing I had left out the last part. But it was hard not to notice.

"You never answered me."

"Pizza," I said.

"You've got a sense of humor. That comes in handy."

"It helps," I said. "I hope it helps."

"But this life's got an even better sense of humor, and the joke's on us." She held her arms out like she was going to do a swan dive, then flapped them as a wrist full of silver bracelets clinked together. "Birds got it made," she said. "But even they've gotta come down sometime."

"They have wings," I said, not sure what that meant, and sure, both at the same time.

"Screw wings," she said, and kicked a rock into the chasm, put her arms down. Took a long deep breath, then let it out. I considered rushing her, but stood there frozen. So much for the action guy I always imagined I'd be. My body was adrenalin-saturated, perhaps enough to pull it off if I lunged. Took my foot off the brakes. Made it happen. But if the timing wasn't perfect...

Then: caution be damned! I came to that: *caution be damned!* I began counting in my head, some primal precursor built into men of action. "Three" would invariably trigger something spring-loaded. At "two," dramatically ringing in my head, a behemoth wearing a biker gang jacket, hair to his shoulders, a single gold earring shimmering, stepped past me and over the low railing.

"There you are, Babe," he said, and she put her arms around his waist. "Some kick-ass view," he said, and she reached up on her tiptoes and kissed him through a thick black beard.

I had a camera on a strap around my neck. I pulled it up, walked a few feet away and began taking snapshots, glanced over furtively when I could. He reached down and squeezed her butt with both hands. Then they climbed back over the railing.

I kept snapping, snapping, not really seeing what was beyond the aperture. No longer seeing what I was seeing. Then I heard in that gravelly voice as they walked off: "Goddamn tourists." And then in that more familiar voice, as the empty spaces blurred: "Assholes," she said.

# The Magician's Lover

She had been sawed in half dozens of times, figuratively and through trickery. Illusions which were never really. The trickery part, she could handle. And now she had his dove. Trained the way she never could be. In her hands. Had that window open: a wide open portal to a wide open sky. When it flew out with a fluttering fury, she slammed the window shut. And her heart slowed a bit. When it circled back, and began tapping a frenzied beak against the glass, its head turned—that single startled eye on her—she knew she was done for.

# Pretty Rain
## (A Micro-Fable)

*O*ne day it rains a pretty rain, and everyone it touches knows beauty. Cars and houses quickly empty. Already attractive people stand in it, naked, against that one gray hair or bit of flab. Plain Janes splash in its puddles with a warrior's cry, erasing the sadness from their cheeks.

*But the next day an ugly rain falls, with disquieting effects. Umbrellas blossom much too late. Forecasters are stumped. People wait indoors with wart-tipped noses against the glass. Which will it be?*

*It's cold as the fat clouds darken. A wise snow comes, weighing on the eaves. Filling the hollows of hats, and slipping into the darkness of high boots, tracked and crunched. A deep snow. A quiet snow, gathering—nearly luminous. Whispering down and landing on wide-eyed faces. And all will have to rethink everything.*

# so much depends…

We sat on a couch for wallflowers who sipped their drinks. She struck me as old-fashioned. Like she would have ridden a bicycle sidesaddle if she could. Outside, a blizzard banged at the windows. I told her I was a writer. She said, *Who isn't?* That she had a cousin who made up names for rodeo bulls. *Chicken on a Chain* was one. Said: *He writes.* The crowd thinned and took much of the body heat with them. She pulled out a joint. Asked what I wrote. When I said poetry, she said, *Who doesn't?*

We smoked it to the nub and went into the kitchen. Put our hands over the red coils of a toaster. Smiling when they touched. She said she had a favorite poem tattooed to her left cheek. Would I like to see it? I said, *Sure.* She lifted her dress, tugged at her panties. And there it was: Williams Carlos Williams' The Red Wheelbarrow. In Courier. Like it was typed there. I was buzzed and the image of the red wheelbarrow and the white chickens seemed so basic, so necessary to me.

*Your turn*, she said, putting herself back together, and our hands rose up again. I considered what it was I had to offer. Gazed out at a landscape losing its color. A snowman gaining way too much weight.

# Smoke Signals

My father would bring home fish instead of flowers, after harsh words stained everything. My mother, watching him from her plastic slipcovers, squeaking on the couch. Blowing cigarette smoke out, hard and fast, in dragon-streams. In a language more facile than words. He'd add the fish to her tropicals. A Kandinsky palette scattering into the water. Roll up his sleeve and reposition the castle, our castle, then pull his arm from the tank. "Your favorites," he'd say, snatching up some tissues and wiping up quickly. My mother's smoke coming out at him in smooth syntax then, thin and measured. Forgiving.

# High Fidelity

It was his idea to wear the blindfolds. Said: Just think how it might enhance our other senses, especially in the sack. Only for today, he said—bumping into walls—never cheating. She wore hers on her head, pretended to knock over things. Moaned with him on top, in high fidelity. Craning her neck, watching TV with the sound off.

# The Grudge Farmer
## (A Micro-Fable)

*H*e wears a red bandana like an outlaw, against a howling stench—a viscous, spitting gall. Tosses them in the back of his pickup. His snarling pit bull, Flash, keeping them from jumping out.

Sells them at a roadside stand beneath a blue umbrella. Someone always stops.

The bastard! The shit! The no-good-cheat! they grumble out of cars: the man in the crushed fedora with a pocketful of band-aids, the woman in the tight capris—the cigarette she flicks, its filter painted Rose Freeze red—another red she's left behind.

The farmer's goods bubble in their muck—the expletives exciting them. Next year, it's yams, the farmer tells himself, slipping on his gloves.

# Mr. Wizard

I was ten when I saw Mr. Wizard shoot down past our window from the sixth floor, that red checkered vest he always wore in a blur. I gasped and pointed. "Mr. Wizard…" I said, barely able to get the words out.

My father was a few feet away talking to a guy in a black leather jacket about a hot TV the man was selling. He said there was a truck outside filled with them. They were going back and forth about the price.

"Not now," my father told me when I persisted. My father knew how to get the price down on anything.

Mr. Wizard was a name my father gave him. Taken from the guy on that TV science show I liked to watch. It stuck. He was a quirky man with a red goatee, and never without that red checkered vest. He was an inventor and the building's misguided Mr. Fixit. My mom would have me ferry a broken toaster or radio up to his apartment. It would come back fine for a week or two, then go on the fritz again. When our toaster finally sparked and went up in flames she cut short those small appliance repair visits. And I wished just once he could get it right because I missed going there. That apartment crowded with oddly shaped contraptions on work benches. A magical place when there was little magic elsewhere to be found.

He had a musical pillow with a recorder in it that had a voice (his) counting sheep, that kept skipping and was too uncomfortable to lay a head on. There was a mechanical back-scratcher with a metal finger at the end of it. He tried, but could never get it to move slowly enough. There was always the threat of impalement.

I never knew where he was from, but Mr. Wizard had a heavy accent. He'd say, "Someday I'm going to win the *Newbell Price.*"

My father plugged in the TV. It was brand new and worked fine when you adjusted the rabbit ears antenna just so.

"*Dad!*" I said.

"Not now," he said. Swung around pointing a finger at me.

I wanted to go to the window and look down. I didn't want to go to the window and look down. I wished my mom were home. She'd listen. I remember her saying Mr. Wizard was a kook. But a kind-hearted one. My dad said he was a know-nothing and left it at that. To me he was the coolest person alive. If only he could get those things to work, he just might have won that Nobel Prize.

There was a comedy show on the new TV and my father handed the man a bunch of bills, and he left.

"I love this show," my father said, putting his arm around me and pulling me into his pride. "Ain't this great?" he said.

I nodded and we both sat on the couch and stared at the screen. I could hear the sirens getting louder, and saw my father turn to listen. Pretty soon everyone in the world would know what I knew. He turned back.

"Get up and move that antenna a little, would ya?" he said. Then, "Boy that's some picture."

# The Small End of the Funnel

P.S. Brenda's doing Phone Sex. Can you believe it? I remember her saying the word "robust" once. It was hot.

P.P.S. Kay's into photography now. Close-ups of rusty staples in phone poles. A red spider on a yellow sponge. Artists. Christ.

P.P.P.S. I called Brenda last night. And man oh man!

P.P. P. P.S. Out of nowhere Kay says, "All cheaters should be pushed down a funnel with the small end in hell." I looked at her like, that's interesting. Like, there's nothing in this fridge worth taking. Only began breathing again when she started taking pictures of the cat.

# Oxalis

We were watching a women's bodybuilding competition on his 13" TV. My father and I in his studio apartment. A couple next door were going at it pretty good, and their bed kept banging against a common wall. My father waved a disapproving hand, said: "Animals!"

"Rabbits, in particular," I said. He lit a cigarette.

"I won on a horse named Satan's Scepter yesterday," he told me. "Go figure—if it was a horse named Angel Harp, I probably would have lost everything." He was tall, my father, and had a bad habit of slumping. Had developed a dowager's hump because of it. He Quasimodoed his way to the wall and pounded. "Give it a rest!" he shouted through the parrot green paint.

I'd come over to tell him Allison and I were splitting up. That no amount of Crazy Glue was going to fix us. And on top of that, I was moving away. Far. Had put in for a transfer nobody wanted. There'd be an ocean between us. He sat back down in that overstuffed chair by the window. The one he sat in when I was growing up—parked in front of the TV—a newspaper always nearby. The control center he barked his edicts from.

"You look good," I told him. He was hunched over. The excessively greased contestants were all on stage now, each doing their individual routines in a posedown. Flexing their freakish proportions, turning this way and that. Their heads too small for their bodies. Smiling for the judges.

"Is that a compliment?" he said. "You giving the old man a compliment? I feel like dog shit."

"Well, you don't look it." I pulled in a kitchen chair and sat beside him. Thought how to tell him. How to begin. He was never one for sharing anything. Anything deeper than a shot of whiskey.

Talked more in metaphors, indirect allusions. Squirmed when you got too personal. For all his bluster, he was eggshell thin when it counted. And didn't want to hear what he didn't want to hear.

I said, "Me and Allison aren't doing so well..." He studied me. A look on his face like he just took something out of the fridge that didn't smell right.

"You wanna keep a car running," he said, "you gotta change the oil. The oil is blood for a car." He turned back. "Look at the ass on that one," he said. "You not only could bounce a quarter off it, the quarter would break into a million pieces." He half laughed.

"Well, anyway, things haven't exactly been going..."

He shouted at the wall again. But the bed kept battering. The contestants were in full swing and my father stooped over further, looking worse than I'd ever seen him.

"Oxalis," he said.

"What?"

"They're weeds. Stubborn little fuckers. You don't keep at it. Pulling them out, pretty soon they'll take over the whole lawn. Kill all the good stuff. The grass, you know?"

"Yeah, sure," I said. "Hey, give me one of those." I hadn't smoked in over a dozen years, but he pulled a cigarette out of the pack and lit it. Reached out.

"I like the one in the blue bathing suit," I told him.

"I like the one in green," he said.

# Late Blooming Gigolo
## (In Triptych)

<u>Scents</u>

He was a professional bingo caller. Had the temperament/ the flair for it. Turned to that gallery of hopefuls with his random edicts. Drawn to Rita (regal Rita) inevitably. Her scents of perfume and want. That pearl necklace and her dignified air. The diamond broach and the voracity with which she laid out so many cards with a widow's privilege. That Siren call: "*Bingo!*"

<u>Cents</u>

He, her Ulysses, sans the rocks to crash against, only that gold in manageable chunks/that want/that fire to warm against. He wouldn't give two cents to change any of it.

<u>Sense</u>

"B-17 , O-23, N-9..."

The scratches into his back, those long candy apple red fingernail markings under his shirt, even when it was so hot his shirt stuck to him, unseen. Their secret.

Earl, whose prior life, so helter-skelter—Big Earl with four firecrackers and a cigarette between his lips, asking for a light. Before. His life, like that. Someone else entirely now. Just a cigarette now at the corner of his mouth. Perhaps one of those fancy French ones which stunk up the room in all the right ways—edgy, Bohemian. And, *Holy Good Lord God Almighty*, his life was finally beginning to make sense.

# Athletic Secrets
## (A Public Service Announcement)

*B*e leery of those secrets that are overly fit. The ones that workout in the dark—deep where the pressure is strongest. All sinew and sadness. That clean and jerk the wee hours over their heads. Do heavy-footed jumping jacks, panting with each count.

Better, the ones that are flimsy and know how to float. The ones that are bubble-bodied, bean-poled—skin and bones. Ones that burn up in sunlight like scrawny slapstick vampires. Ones made of fog and smoke—a good stiff wind can blow away.

# The Mountain That Spit Up Pianos
## (A Micro-Fable)

*L*osing faith in all things magical, a man scoffed when he heard there was a small island, with a volcano at the center of it, that spit up pianos in a continuous stream—each landing delicately upright, ready to be played.

Cynical, but eager to disprove the outrageous claim, he journeyed to that meager bit of real estate. And there, after a short trek, found the island's singular mountain spewing one piano after another in a tumbling downpour, landing delicately all around him.

The man watched for some time with his jaw swung open, not in wonder, but in head-shaking disbelief that he had traveled so far for such an empty moment. Throwing up his hands dismissively he headed back to the boat, back home—eager to tell everyone, anyone who would listen, how they were all spinets. "Spinets, damn it!—and not a single baby grand among them!"

# A Visit to the Nervous Hospital

P.S. I visited Amy today at the Nervous Hospital. (That's what she calls it). She says, Hi – sort of.

P.P.S. She still insists that there are "forces" that want to turn them all into rubber duckies, so they can take complete control. She says they have a giant bathtub filled with water on the third floor. That they have them float around in circles all day. That the water is never changed. I can't tell if she is speaking metaphorically or believes it.

P.P.P.S. Can you imagine? It was so upsetting. I still have that book of poems she wrote. They're so beautiful they make me weep. Where the hell is she anyway?

P.P.P.P.S. The nurse came by with her meds while I was there. It was like a pharmacy for one. So colorful. Like the M&Ms we used to eat as kids.

P.P.P.P.P.S. I miss her!

P.P.P.P.P.P.S. I asked if there was anything she liked about this place and she said, "Yes, the red jello." I said, "Great." She said, eating it she felt like a little bird sipping a crocodile's tears.

P.P.P.P.P.P.P.S. Fuck!

P.P.P.P.P.P.P.P.S. I smiled, sort of, and she smiled, sort of, back. And for a moment I thought she might even be there. Sort of.

# Dragonfly in Lieu of a Chopper

They were on the roof of their house and they saw a dead cow and a few cars rush by in the flood waters. She was hugging their cat and she and her husband were searching the sky for a rescue helicopter. When she lowered her eyes to comfort the cat she saw the dragonfly with its herky-jerky air-play, hover, then whiz by.

A week earlier she was terribly upset that those shoes she'd ordered online didn't fit right, and she'd have to pack them up and head on over to the post office. Now, what post office? Where?

He took his jacket off and put it around her shoulders. Curling into the animal, she took it off and wrapped the cat in it. The dragonfly flew back again showing off, perhaps, its prowess for flight, or maybe it was looking for answers. Where the hell was that creek it was so fond of? The mosquitos it picked off...?

She peered up at her husband, who still had his head in the sky. And for an instant, a fraction of one, she stopped listening for the sound of those chopper blades whipping the air closer, tugged on his pant leg. Said, hoping somehow it would matter, even a little: "She's purring."

# A Piece of Sky

Crossing the street on the way to his place, he noticed a few puzzle pieces scattered in the gutter. One, a squiggle of bright sky, pressed into a patch of roadwork tar. *Black and blue*, he told her. *It's kind of beautiful.*

*What's so beautiful about black and blue? That's just plain weird*, she said, worrying a silver Scottie dog on a charm bracelet he'd given her. He had a walk-in closet they were heading toward, lined with aluminum foil and heat lamps. Pots of marijuana at its center, in a manicured flourish. He'd clip some buds for her, and they'd make love. Then he'd get ready for work. His swing shift at the U.S. Mint where, with a great machine, he'd punch the numismatic heads of presidents into coins. Again and again. Somebody else's money. Getting dressed, he watched her slipping into a pair of blue panties. Thought of that sliver of sky again, pressed into the tar. How pretty it was. How pretty enough it was.

# The Limits of Art
## (A Micro-Fable)

*L*ooking in the mirror, he sees a colossal flare of peacock feathers fan out behind him. Wow! He races to the Bottoms Up Club down the street, his folded plumes dragging behind him. If he can't score now, he thinks—he might as well hang it up.

It's packed inside with lots of women. He goes to the jukebox, slips in a coin, and lets 'er rip—a feathery splendor slowly spreading nearly to the ceiling. The music comes on, and he does this little dance incorporating a quiver to the plume tips, which is apparently irresistible because five beauties, who wouldn't give him a hint of a tumble, minutes prior, surround him cooing—their painted lips coquettishly parted.

Left, right—quiver, quiver—left, right… He's in the zone, when suddenly a fight breaks out. Two guys across from them, playing rough. One pulls back his sweatshirt hood, revealing a large pair of ram's horns: the other, the same. His fickle bevy scatter, reassemble for a closer look. Each man now on either end of the room, head down, poised to rocket.

He needs a drink, shuffles off, his long train trailing in the sawdust.

"What's your poison?" the barkeep says, above some puffy squeals—the clash, the thunder.

# The Need to Know

My wife wakes up and goes, first thing, to her *Dream Log*. Makes an entry. Google-crazed, she's been looking for meanings. Scrambled metaphors translated into something accountable. Making sense of nonsense. So much mud and mulch stuffed in. Strange alphabets and snapped off parts of things.

"What?" I ask, my boner with nowhere to go.

She's clicking/typing/scrolling.

"Come back to bed."

"A scarecrow," she says, "in a field of pincushions. At least I think they were. Not sure, but I'm going with pincushions. And it was giving a kind of soliloquy. Can you imagine?"

"Wait. The pincushion?"

"You're not listening," she says. "The scarecrow. You must be horny." I haven't a clue what I dream most times. And when I do, two seconds later it's evaporating mist. And I'm wishing her computer would do the same. It's toasty hot under these covers. And who gives a damn anyway what a scarecrow's got to say. "Fucking crows!" probably. "Fucking crows!" Or, "I'd give a bucket of straw to hop off this pole. For a quick roll in the hay." I could easily imagine.

# Stuntman in Still Life

He says he died in half a dozen or so movies: shot in the back, running through the woods on fire, pushed off a roof... Says, Marilyn Monroe kissed him once on his bald head. Kept those hot lipstick lips there till they finally wore off on their own.

He sits at Hurley's Tavern now, and even at his advanced age, can drop from the stool with his face all twisted like he'd just been shot if you tell him a joke with a corny punchline.

Says, he prays to Saint Kick-In-The-Pants, the patron saint of fuck-ups, and he's still waiting to hear back.

Says, actresses these days get puffy lip injections. But Marilyn had 'em natural.

Says, "Did I ever tell you about that chase scene I did in San Francisco? Up and down those goddamn crazy hills?"

Says, he could rip a phonebook in half when he was twelve. A page at a time.

Says, he was an expert at predicting the past. It was his specialty.

Says, "They gave my Millie a fifty-fifty chance and she got the fifty alright. Only it was the wrong one."

Says, "Hey, you watering down this shit or what? Give me a double, you big bag of wind, and fill it up like you mean it this time."

# Sonic Boom

"An airplane is like a blister on the heavens," he said, looking up. "Get a grip," she said. "This garden isn't going to plant itself." There were two saplings angled against the fence, a wheelbarrow filled with perennials. He picked the trowel up, plunged it into the soil. Some personalities were so large they dispersed another's language altogether, he thought. Left it to languor in the lungs. She handed him some bulbs. "How deep do you want these holes?" he asked. She demonstrated without speaking. And when she turned, he noticed her shadow fill an empty bucket to the brim.

# Whiteout

They were in his studio. A room that was to be their first-born's. When it was thought possible. When it seemed so many things were. She was studying to become a nurse now. Had a plastic liver in her hand from an anatomical torso on a table a room away. He had called her in, threw his hands up, pointing at his new painting like a car showroom model.

"Wow," she said—that vague and noncommittal expletive hanging there. It was another of his comical tampon paintings. (Though bloodless, she found them more than mildly distasteful.) There was a plethora of them against and on the wall. They flew over buildings with little wings, were a tampon forest under a purple sky, swam upstream like salmon, arched and over-bright... The walls (not pink nor blue) were blizzard white.

"A spleen?" he said.

"A liver," she told him.

He had an eye that went rogue and turned in when he got excited. He had a prism in his eyeglasses that corrected the defect, but rarely wore them anymore. She gazed at the painting for a moment, then beyond it, snow-blinded for a time.

"I've got to get back," she said, as he straightened the canvas (a cityscape logjam of tampon taxis with tiny wheels). Stood back for the longshot, cocking his head, this way and that.

She returned the liver to its slot. Sat down in front of a note-book and a pile of books. Removed the heart from the plastic torso with a jeweler's precision. Held it, bloodless and stopped, thought: *how perfect it looked that way.*

# Sewn In

Outside the diner it was raining. Periodically, a truck's air brakes would add its hiss to the mix. The trip had been tough. Talk, cracked as some of those roads. There were miles yet. Rain shadows ran down that dress you got in Mexico. Little mirror pieces sewn in. You said, "We are all prisoners of our own momentum." I passed the salt. Didn't know what else to do. The waitress poured coffee like she invented it. Had a wet rag that did little more than reconfigure the table grease. When she flipped her pad page over, we looked up.

# Erasure

Janelle still had her ex-pimp's name, over a smoking gun tattoo, peeking out of her blouse. *Property of "Stinger"*. She had been out of the life for years. Many states away. Living in her brother's basement. Writing country songs she sang at the *Bottom Rung*. With a beer at her feet she lifted often. The bartender's name was Rusty. But he wasn't. She didn't know which of his lava lamps she liked best. He never asked about her tattoos. One night they went back and forth like kids. "Bet you can't"/"Bet I can…" "Holy-goddamn-god-almighty," he said, when she did.

# The Sin Suit
## (A Micro-Fable)

*I*t took years to develop: hand-lined with sin magnets (rife with the finest draw-worthy proclivities). It was cloud-whisper white. He strutted in it through the town, lifting the sins from passers-by, their cluttered vaults/ unwashable hands.

After the first day's stroll the suit darkened. By midweek, transgressions poked through like springs in a shabby hotel mattress, with a dank, tarry drip.

The fast-good people took to playing bingo in church basements and checkers online, with ennui closing in, showing its teeth.

Cults of fallen goody two-shoes huddled around it/him—their new prophet. Young housewives ran their hands through the suit's folds, down a trouser crease, sighing with each scoop of dirt under their nails. Pleading for a few naughty returns.

"Sure, sure," he said, stepping back, something swift and shivery slipping under his lapel. "But it'll cost ya."

# Ketchup

P.S. Bobby's been filling his pockets lately with little packets of ketchup and taking them to school. I asked him why. He said if a shooter comes shooting up the place he's going to lie down and squeeze them all over himself so it looks like he's been shot, so the shooter will think he's dead and move on. Can you imagine? Whatever happened to just reading, writing and 'rithmatic? Chrissake!

P.P.S. The other night I saw him in bed with one of those inflatable globes. I asked him if he was planning on going somewhere. He was staring at it and moving his finger from one country to another. He just ignored me. I'm starting to really worry about him.

P.P.P.S. When you get back let's talk about a head doctor. I know you're not too keen on the idea, but this is a new reality we're living in with all these shootings. We can't continue to look away.

P.P.P.P.S. On a lighter note, and Lord knows we need one, the other day I put on my glasses and saw something out of the corner of my eye. It was a tiny spider swinging down on a thread or whatever it is they swing down on. You know how much I hate spiders but this one was cute. It made me a little sad when I had to squish it and ball it up in a tissue. But little spiders grow up to be big spiders. And we can't have that. So I guess this wasn't a happy note after all. But it sure was sweet for a hot minute, so there's that.

# Voice-overs

They watched the old casino go down. The synchronized explosives giving the illusion it was slowly sinking into the earth. "I loved that friggin' place," the father said, staring into the pall and rubble. They hadn't seen each other in over six years. But after the father buried his third wife (the other two still blowing cigarette smoke at their TVs and cursing him) he called his eldest to meet him in Las Vegas. Said he felt lucky. Lucky enough for the both of them.

His dad was wearing a silk shirt and those horrible white pants when they met up later at the *Flamingo*. There was so much the son wanted to tell him: how he skydived for the first time. Walked the earth a little differently now that he wasn't smeared across it. A bit more restlessly perhaps. How he was taking a class. Making musical instruments out of found objects. A motor oil can guitar you could actually play. He was learning to play. How he wanted to quit his job at the plant, do voice-overs for a living: cartoons and TV commercials. How Vicky said he was good at it (when he wasn't overdoing it and driving her nutty). That the couples counseling, this time, was helping.

But when he quipped a few times in a Donald Duck voice or an exaggerated super hero baritone, his father just gazed at him as though his eyes had suddenly crossed or turned a different color. Said nothing, just ordered another drink. Then: "You need to be soused to enjoy Vegas."

At the crap table his father drew a crowd. Winning at first, betting big—his colorful urgings with each release of the dice causing laughter. Sweet-talking them as they rattled in his loose fist, till his luck ran out, and he was just an old man again, spilling his drink onto his spit-shined loafers.

In the restroom, the son held him up as he puked into the sink. Tried once more to make a joke of it with a silly voice. His father looked up, smiled this time. "That's good," he said. "Reminds me of what's his face? On TV. You know—what's his face?"

"That's him," the son said in his real voice, taking a paper towel to his father's chin. His real voice becoming more and more unfamiliar to him, considerably less interesting.

# Straight to It

He lives a life pursued in continuous circles, or more accurately, ovaloids. Drives an ice truck at a skating rink a town over. Layer upon layer, Hard and quick-drying. Bundles up for the job.

Unbundles for his TV dinners, his TV. Fully, for the youngish divorcee down the hall. Who knocks lightly. Brings him Chinese takeout to complement his bottle of E & J. Settles on a couch with yellow flowers his ex picked out years earlier. The couch with four wooden feet nailed mercifully by gravity to the rug. Bouncy, but stable, where melting is a plus now, circling a minus.

# Geisha

He puts an ad in the paper for a geisha. It is the wet, mushy center of a New York summer, and she arrives breezy at his door in a gauzy outfit and zombie-faced with bone-white greasepaint in contrast to glossy candy apple-red lipstick. When he requests a fan dance, she grabs up a small electric fan from the kitchen table. Asks if he has an extension cord, which he does. She has him take off his trousers and lie down on the couch in his tighty-whities. She edges up close, with a little hip wiggle and shoulder roll, and runs the frisky air up and down him. Sings a Lady Gaga song he doesn't recognize, and dances to it.

• • •

For the tea ceremony she uses Lipton while he waits so long for it to chill in the frosted glasses from the freezer, that he turns on the TV and watches the news. They sit on the couch and drink it. Make several toasts back and forth, the ice cubes nearly spilling over the top. She, continually filling his glass every time it lowers an inch or two. And he, excusing himself to go to "The little boy's room."

• • •

When asked to read him some poetry, she bows and recites a couple of dirty limericks she used to hear her drunken father recite, with a slurred and salacious bravado at family get-togethers.

• • •

He is happy to see she is comely, when she steps from the bathroom with her make-up off, and is delighted to find she likes a lot of the same TV shows he does. Later in the evening, they perform fan dances for each other to his Elvis records. Only once, when they become overly adventurous, pulling the plug from the wall.

# Saw Blade

I talk Nina into it; Ed goes along. Neither can figure why I'm still pining over Rita.

The three of us have a musical saw band. Pass the hat most times. Carry around these small collapsible garden seats. Sit under Rita's window, the saws between our knees, bending and bowing Rita's favorite: *Head Like A Hole.*

Her window's open and I'm hoping she'll find the sorrowful tones, the sweet sentiment, irresistible. But I'm beginning to think she's not home, till it starts raining some of my paperbacks. Troopers that we are, we keep playing. One by one they're flying out. And then this shirtless guy with a plethora of angry animal tattoos sticks his head out, says, "Get lost you crazy fucks!" as a hand snakes around his waist and eases him back in. The fingernails painted *Cayenne Pepper Red.* Rita's favorite go-to shade.

We stop and Nina picks up one of the books, coos: "*Baudelaire.* Can I have it?"

I nod and we pack up. *Los Guanacos* is a couple of streets down and if the mariachis aren't there, we've got a spot.

Nina looks at me as we head off, Baudelaire in a reverential clutch. "Nothing like a saw," she says. "to cut through all the bullshit."

# A Change of Clothes

*W*idows are beautiful, he thought. So covered in need they shimmered. This was his second. She lay under a sheet, which had a hole burnt through it earlier, from the pot seeds that popped from a fat joint. *His suits suit you*, she said. *A little tight in the shoulders, but not bad.* Her cat rubbed against his leg, as if nothing had changed. He turned this way and that in the long mirror. She rolled another, using a credit card to separate the seeds out this time.

# Rhapsody of Fallen Objects
## (A Public Service Reminder)

*Sometimes when enough has fallen down around you, it becomes a music you can dance to. Glass objects separating like startled birds across the hardwood floor. The thud of weightier things, dented but not broken. A makeshift orchestra gravity conducts. As you go about the business of the day—the pieces oddly melodic. Something you can tap a foot to.*

# A Different Song

The mockingbird is out there again, imitating her cat in heat. An unsettling repertoire, Susan thinks. Days earlier, it was content mimicking other birds. One golden oldie after another, silencing a tree full of them.

She's wearing a wig with bowl-cut bangs, applies some Devil's Blush Red lipstick and rubs on wild circles of rouge. Is *Gloria*. She is years younger and her husband is not a pastor. The kids aren't grown, aloof—scattered here and there.

She sits at the kitchen table and hitches up her skirt against the heat.

He was a criminal and the trial went on forever. As reprehensible a soul in deeds as he is a poet on the page. She reads his letter again, then folds and slips it into her bra. Later she will add it to the others in her hiding place along with everything else. She bends over a sheet of perfumed stationary, one arm sticking to a placemat. The window fan/the mocking bird, white noise now. There is so much she wants to say. Gloria wants to tell him.

# A Thing with Feathers

I come home to find a pile of ashes smoldering in the tub. Figure it is all that is left of my father. My mother is sitting on the toilet lid, smoking. Staring down at the pile, misty-eyed.

With all that drinking, it was bound to happen. *Spontaneous combustion* is more common than you think. A gut full of booze, every pore floating in it. One match too close to a half-smoked cigarette, and *Poof!* I guess she didn't know where else to put him.

"Dad?" I ask, thinking, spontaneous combustion must be a pallbearer's dream.

"Dad, what?"

"Dad?" I repeat, pointing.

"No. Our divorce papers," she says. "I never signed the damn things. He's quit the booze. Is in AA regular now."

"And you believe him?"

She shrugs. "He's landed a job at *Scallywags*, tending, and is taking me out to *Villa Romana* tonight. When's the last time he did that?"

"*Scallywags?*" I say. "Why not just give him an IV and hook it up to a brewery?"

"Always the cynic. Have a little faith." She lifts the lid and lets the cigarette hiss out in the bowl. Reaches over with her free hand and turns on the faucet, splashes some water onto the pile. "Here," she says, handing me a dustpan. "Help me clean up this mess."

"Sure," I tell her—grab the pan and scoop up the ashes. Decide Dickinson had it right: "Hope is a thing with feathers..." Take the soggy mush, mulch now, out into the garden where the roses are waiting.

# The Viking and the Elephant Trainer's Great-Great Grandson

His "client" says, "I did the family tree thing and found out I'm descended from the Vikings. Can you believe it?"

"Kind of cool," Jake says. "As long as there's no rape and pillaging involved." His client laughs, the comment being particularly ironic, since he is in a wheelchair and Jake is the person who delivers his medical marijuana.

They are sampling it. The client seems pleased. There is a light in his eyes that wasn't there when Jake first arrived. Jake doesn't know if it is the fact that his client has company or if it is "the product." Maybe both.

"I got one of those goofy Viking hats online, with the horns on the sides. Want me to break it out?"

"I'll take a raincheck," Jake says.

"My great-great grandfather was an elephant trainer for the circus," Jake  says, not sure why. He knows absolutely nothing about anyone in his family that far back.

"Really," the client says, rolling the wheelchair a bit closer and offering the joint.

Jake waves him off gently. "Got some more deliveries yet. You go ahead."

There's a TV on with the sound off. They stare for a moment at footage on a news station of a woman dropping a baby from the window of a burning building into the arms of a man below. It is a jittery cellphone video and they keep replaying it in slow motion.

When they go to commercial, the client says, "No way I could deal with all that poop."

"Huh?"

"The elephant poop."

"Oh, yeah, mountains." Jake laughs. Hopes it doesn't come off as fake. Thinks the word "poop" is charming, coming from a Viking. He thinks to make a joke about giant elephant diapers but says instead. "I'll look forward to seeing you in that hat next time."

"Count on it," the client says. Holds up what is left of the joint. "Hey, this is some good shit."

"You bet," Jake says and is already thinking about Mrs. Meyers (his next delivery) and her dog stories. Then he thinks, why an elephant trainer? Then, that was one hell of a catch that guy made with that baby. Then, looks at his watch, furtively.

His client pays him and places the prized stash in his pajama pocket, rolls his way over to the door.

Jake follows, says, "That was some catch."

"Nice when it works out that way. I hope they replay it later."

"I'm sure they will," Jake says. Then thinks, I hope he forgets about wearing the hat with the horns. Then, I hope nobody stole my bike. Then, I'm running behind, so many more deliveries. Then, I wonder if Tracey is really going to leave me. Then, I'll get her flowers. Then, yeah, a lot of good that's going to do. Then, *Christ*, was it irises or lilies she liked so much, I keep forgetting.

"Okay, so no plundering, right?" Jake says.

"No plundering," the Viking assures, closing the door behind the elephant trainer's great-great grandson.

# Stuffed

We're old school, us clowns, folded up inside the gutted out VW bug, just right. No trapdoor under the car, like some think, for an endless bunch of us to climb into a false bottom, then step out cool as shit one after another in unimaginable numbers—the kids squealing, their parents oohing and aahing.

We're a puzzle of folded limbs and torsos we've perfected like they did building the pyramids. You couldn't slide a credit card between us.

"You cut a butt bomb, you're dead," Pete says.

"Likewise," Allen tells him. And it's all in good fun.

But not me and Mel. Not even close. I know he's been cozying up to Sheila lately, that trick-rider I've been seeing. He and me are pressed together like two jigsaw pieces and I'm digging an elbow into his ribs. I've got a few muscles under this getup and I'm giving it to him good. And he knows he's got it coming and doesn't cry out. You can almost see the blood rushing to his face under all that make-up.

"You get my drift?" I tell him.

"I can't breathe," he says.

"Good," I tell him, "remember the feeling."

He nods. "Okay," he whispers, straining to speak. I hope for his sake he means it.

A few of the fellas have already climbed out and things are loosening up. As each of us exits the ringmaster counts into his mic with the audience counting along. It's nearly my turn and I give him one last poke for good measure and he groans.

"*Sev-en!*" I hear as I set foot in the ring with a goofy smile and waving my arms, despite the stiffness. The kids are so excited. It never gets old. The higher the number, the louder they get.

Sheila's up next and I see her in the wings. She gives me a wink. She's wearing that skimpy blue outfit I love. I shoot her a smile even bigger than the one that's painted on.

# Gun with a Conscience
## (A Micro-Fable)

*A*man invents a gun with a conscience. It fits in the hand with a sigh and you can feel it squirm. He hasn't worked out all the kinks, however. It still will kill anyone—innocent bystanders: the child, mid-step about to board a bus, the old woman through the wall of her kitchen as she counts her change. All gunpowder, velocity and intrusion.

Yet still, he is hopeful—for the bullets all come out of the barrel weeping.

# Side Effects

You may experience wanting to use your father's gold cufflinks, but do not have a shirt with the little cuff slits to accommodate them. You may find yourself wearing his severely starched white shirt (one of several his fifth and last wife sent you after he passed) to the new acting class you are taking. Even when you are offering your kingdom up for a horse. Even when you are yelling, "Stella! HEY, STELLAAAAA!!!" into a sweltering New Orleans night.

• • •

It's been reported one may miss the smell of nail polish, from time to time. Think of her applying it. That little brush dipped in, dipped out. A shade called, Devil's Sunburn Red. Transforming ordinary fingernails into five rubies in a setting as she lifts a glass of water to her lips.

• • •

You may recall your father's use of the word "wiseacre" while you are watching a performance in class, massacring a scene that you know you could do better. How your father would say it when you got a phrase right on *Wheel of Fortune* well before half the letters were lighted up in that elegant manner by a young and classy Vanna White. How he told you, sotto voce, she was the only reason he watched. Then, that corny and indirectly praise-ready word again: "Wiseacre" when you figured out the next one. How warm it felt, like a freshly ironed shirt you put on quickly, before the heat has a chance to escape.

• • •

A heightened sensitivity to sound is less common, but possible. One of the actors might tell you with bluster and a straight face that he is a descendant of the devil. And when you stare at him as though he is a chin-high pile of horse shit, he might insist: "No, *really*. Not the Devil himself, but a minor one. I did a family tree search with this expert, and he narrowed it down to the foothills of Potenza. That's in Italy." His eyes are piercing, laser-darting. "Exorcisms run in my family." Then his tight and earnest expression might suddenly come apart. "Ha-ha-ha... Had you, didn't I?"

You may experience an augmenting, but unacted upon lunge and throat clutch, followed by a fake laugh you've perfected. You might snap out of it, realizing you'll be reading your part next after the break.

• • •

It is not uncommon to feel a variation of that "warm shirt" validating sensation when a lovely woman with purple lipstick tells you you're brilliant and invites herself to your place to study lines. A few drinks later deciding clothes are extraneous, so you shed them and discover she is covered in tattoos. You might easily get lost in them. But it is also a "lost & found" and you grasp more and more elements of what have been found. Feel how smooth her skin is, even over that small mountain range, that scaly dragon's tail... Find your breath again, afterward, as you share a joint (your first in many years). Maybe your first ever.

• • •

Other possible reactions may include: a keen sense that gravity has an "off" button. That laughing (honest laughing) is like riding a bike. That daylight can go on vacation, can return home again. That home can return home again—even to another location, and still be home. While studying lines together you might notice her nail polish bejeweling the page. Discover, you are both *wiseacres* in the making.

# Strangers in a Strange Land

She said she remembered ice boxes. Before there were refrigerators. Big blocks of ice that kept the food from rotting. Said the mob controlled even that. Controlled water. "Can you believe it?" she said.

My mother was in the bed across from her (a new arrival) asleep with her mouth open. It wasn't a pretty picture. But she survived the hospital and now I was here to cheerlead her on to surviving this nursing home.

"And I miss the old TVs," she went on. "The snow even. Can you imagine missing such a thing? That static when the stations went off the air. It put me to sleep. Better than the pills they give in this place," my mom's roommate said. The old woman with the blue hair and a lop-sided smile. There was a picture of her young and beautiful in sepia framed on a dresser.

"Your mom's a kicker," she said. "Doesn't say much, but the few stories she did tell me—*momma mia*."

I tried to imagine what she could have meant. Was there a plumber with thick hands that grabbed more than a rusty pipe, or some secret lover I never knew about? Alone all day with Albert, her canary, and Fritz, our German shepherd. Two loyals that would never snitch.

I glanced at her photo again. Thought how you sometimes meet an old person and think they were born that way. All you know of them. I thought of an iceman walking up the stairs of an old building. A brute with big shoulders and a pair of tongs. I pictured an old console TV with a tiny screen set in it like a jewel. I'm old enough to remember the static when the transmissions ended. The handful of stations back then. "The snow" —a noisy blizzard, swimming dots in black and white.

I imagined her on the couch, an empty glass on an end table, lipstick on the rim. A bottle. High heels on the floor. Hats on a hall tree. There were always hats back then and the smell of cigarettes. A man with his hair slicked back with scented grease says, "Hey, babe..." to the woman in the photo. She stretches out. He's wearing a tie and loosens it. A noose from work he can remove. "Come 'ere, handsome," she says, whether or not he is. He approaches...

My mom woke. "Well nice talking to you," I said to her blue hair, at a part of it I noticed was standing straight up.

"Likewise," she said and sank back into her pillow.

My mom, who is legally blind, yawned, said, "Ricky, is that you?" There's a photo of her on a little dresser as well. The same sepia-smooth perfection — forever young.

"It's me," I said. Walked the long, hard miles to her end of the room.

# Skyped

All those concerts she never saw, that handprint spackled over with make-up, the halter tops he threw out with the left over mashed potatoes and those dry veggie stars the cat wouldn't eat are in that smile, as she sits on the edge of the bed—five states between them—a naked stranger beside her waving, fish-eyed on the screen, toasting up a bottle of gin.

*"Hi Dad."*

# Time Machine

They have the entire back seat of his old Impala in their living room. All that sex, the big talks/those telescopic musings/pot/cigarette smoke curling against the windows...

Now all that is necessary is a pulse and the ability to fog a mirror he jokes. They still laugh a lot, but stop when their old Chihuahua, Mighty Joe Young, poops on the seat beside them as they're watching TV. They are stoned and look at each other without words in mutual telepathic pleading, till he relents, gets the *409* and cleans up.

He works the lights at a local theater house and she takes the tickets. Their lives compressed and convenient in that way. The old Chihuahua is a stand-in for the kids they could never have; the parrot, two cats and fish tank bubbling in their bedroom, as well.

Every so often, she wears that yellow Mexican dress with the vibrating red roses when he is sitting there in his boxer shorts, and hops on board. That back seat time machine (duct taped a bit) still holding up.

# The King of Non Sequiturs

He was the King of Non Sequiturs. She'd unceremoniously dubbed him that long ago. They'd been together for nearly thirty years. Sunlight lay on the kitchen table between them. Mostly on the monthly bills she was doing. Her thick fingers pounding that small calculator.

"What's this $19.99 for?"

"An infomercial," he said. "I forget what it was. Some thing-amajig or other." He sipped his coffee.

"More crap," she said. "We don't need more crap."

"You know," he mused, "I've always wondered what it would be like to be a reindeer herder. Maybe paddle in a boat made of walrus skin in the Bering Sea."

"Okay, Santa, how about this other $19.99?"

"Same," he said. "It was late. They all sound like something you can't live without when it's late."

"Money is something we can't live without," she told him. One of the bills slipped from the table and he got up and bent to get it. He was afflicted with "Plumber's Butt"—the crack of which peeked up at her. She shook her head and said thanks as he sat back down with it.

"I could sell my hats at the flea market," he said. He was bald and his hat collection was vast.

"You're moving in the right direction," she said. "And don't forget we've got dinner at the Berman's tonight."

"No problem," he said.

He began folding the bill he'd retrieved in odd ways. She leaned back and watched him.

70

"I wonder if you can make an origami sandpiper," he said. "Or a peach tree. Wouldn't that be something?" She snatched it back from him and smoothed it out.

"Oh, okay," he said. He got up and poured a fresh cup for the two of them, wondering the whole time what it might be like pushing off from shore and rowing like mad in the Bering Sea in a walrus-skin boat. His reindeer herd, on the icy bank, watching him get smaller and smaller.

# The Metamorphosis Revisited

He awakes to find he is a thingamajig. Some indeterminable gizmo. There is a cog (of sorts) where his stomach should be. Oddly enough it growls.

"Holy crap!" he says, looking into the dresser mirror.He clinks out to the kitchen where his wife is sipping her coffee and reading the paper. He has a crank and a nondescript lever, a doohickey of some kind with a flexible joint; he points at himself. "Meg," he says, "what the hell?"

His wife looks up and appraises him. "Hmm," she says. "I wonder what that Finnegan pin does. This might not be so bad, Fred–depending."

"Depending?" he screeches. "Depending on what?"

"Well, you never know what might come in handy. It might take some time to figure it all out. But, I think you've got a lot of potential here."

"But I'm a…whatchamacallit."

She reaches over and presses a button. Something begins turning, a bit squeakily. "A little oil can fix that," she says. "You know, let's not be negative. I bet you'll come in handy in ways you can't even imagine."

He sits his thingamabob nondescript form down across from her. "I suppose," he says. "Actually, I never felt better. Hand me the crossword." And she slides it over. A long doo-dad reaches out and grabs it.

# Ballet, Sinus Headaches, and a Decent Steak

Sandra performed water ballet. Legs bending, twirling. There'd been talk of the Olympics. But her sinuses betrayed her. Those synchronized legs in a team photo, glistening. The machinery, she'd describe, at work below the art. I thought, isn't that the way it is? So many cogs even for the simplest graces. She married a butcher after we split up. He got her sinus meds. Watched films of her young legs breaking the water. She told me she was happy. Didn't miss any of it. I listened for machinery: clanking, hums. Didn't hear it. She said, the meat was always fresh.

# The Mermaid and the Laughing Santa

P.S. Far as the blahs I was telling you about last time, things are picking up. Me and Jeff went to this laugh therapy class the doc recommended. This roly-poly guy that runs it looks like Santa without the red suit. Says we all need to yuck it up a lot more. That it relieves stress. Even if you're not in the mood.

P.P.S. Still got the blahs but not so bad and a long blond mermaid wig Jeff got me. And *holy cow!* It's making a *big* difference if you get my drift.

P.P.P.S. Thanks for sending those pics of you and Carl. Wow! Alaska! Glad to know you two weren't trampled by that herd of moose or is it mooses. HA HA!

P.P.P.P.S. My Joey's been watching Ancient Aliens on TV lately. That creepy show. The things they come up with. Like I don't have enough on my plate with dragging him to soccer practice, Jeff's drinking, and me having my hair falling out from the treatments without thinking about what else might be out there.

P.P.P.P.P.S. Anyways hope you guys get a kick out of the pic of me in the mermaid wig with Jeff giving me the finger horns like a goofy teenager. I've been wearing it around the house so be prepared when you visit. And don't be freaked out by all the laughing even when it doesn't make any sense. It's really helping I think. Yeah. No it really is.

# A Horse with a Fork in Its Head
## (A Micro-Fable)

*After the revolution, it is taught in all the schools that a horse with a fork in its head is a unicorn.*

*The teachers all wear uniforms with creases sharp as knives. Their cheeks plump and overstuffed like suitcases that will not close. And hardly ever do.*

*When your feet get stuck in mud, they say, it simply means: the earth is your new pair of shoes.*

# Talking Dummies

She was at the bar drinking a Brandy Alexander, when the men on either side of her began making their respective moves. It had been a long week, and she had her high heels off, her stocking feet dangling.

The one on her right had the unnerving habit of dramatizing a moment like a mock coming attractions announcer: *See the stunning woman lift her drink to the finest lips on earth, her bracelets sliding down her lovely arm. A thing of unimaginable beauty!*

"Sounds like a carnival barker's pitch," she said, and he laughed, slinging down another shot. He was handsome, she thought, and probably drove a car symbolically long and expensive.

On her left was a gentleman, a decade older, who talked in excited bursts about a chain of businesses he owned. They each, interchangeably, were buying her drinks which the barkeep (a close friend) was watering down.

She viewed the men on either side of her as ventriloquists' dummies for their talking penises. Once the starch was out of them, they'd be doubled over, silent, like any other dummy. But for now they were perky and loquacious. The drinks were free and steady, and if she had to be one of those bobblehead dolls for a time—what the hell?

After *last call*, Pete, the bartender, would shut the place down and drive her home. He was into Feng Shui, and was giving her tips on how to rearrange the furniture. It was calming, she felt, the way he did it. Each item in its place. Whether or not it made a gnat's worth of difference, she didn't know or care. It worked.

He'd sit in the tub with her and rub her feet, listen to her complain about her boss, the accounts files piled to the ceiling. And sometimes they'd smoke pot. When it came time for Pete's penis to do the talking (and eloquent it was) she'd be all ears.

76

# The Old Woman and
# Her Breezy Blue Islands

See an old woman in bed staring at the wallpaper: a washed-out floral pattern with fleur-de-lis borders  A pattern her grandmother picked out when it was in fashion. The old woman is on her last legs and the TV, this wicked wall covering, are all she has to gaze upon.

• • •

Hear her call out to her son, who is living off disability checks and her Social Security, sitting in the kitchen carving sexually explicit, and primitively rendered wooden figures he is copying from the Kamasutra he has laid out on the kitchen table. They are for an art exhibit in a local coffeehouse where a shelf has been cleared for them. A show he will call: "Horny Wood." See him standing there at her bedside holding his whittling knife. Hear her tell him: "Either I go or that God-awful wallpaper does. And I ain't going first!"

• • •

See her looking through several wallpaper sample books, and her face brighten as she settles on one in particular. See the back of the paperhanger's broad plaid shirt, which is what she sees. See a breezy blue image emerge. An ever expanding fresco of small boats with sails billowed. Tiny islands with a single coco-nut-laden palm tree on each. Little V's which are seagulls swirl-ing overhead she can hear.

• • •

Hear Fred, the old woman's son, on the phone with his girl-friend Gloria, telling her she just "doesn't get him." She is a hair stylist who works out of her kitchen, one of the few things they have in common aside from excellent make up sex. She tells him she doesn't want any of her friends seeing "That smut!"

"You wouldn't know great art if it jumped up and bit you on the bosom," he tells her.

"Bosom?" she says. "Really—*bosom?*"

"Oh, hell," he says and hangs up.

• • •

See the old woman take the TV remote, from amongst a miniature Stonehenge of pill bottles, and click off the set.

See her young again with William back at the helm. Those strong hands with wispy black hairs along the knuckles. They are heading for an island. They have wine (a rare and wonderful vintage) and a blanket to spread out. They will island-hop, caress under every swaying palm.

• • •

See Fred gather up all the wood shavings and put them in a bag. He thinks of them as *unart*—what he has cut away to set the true art free. Late at night, as his mother snores two rooms over, he will toss them bit by bit into the fireplace. Watch them spark and glow only for an instant, then turn to ash.

• • •

Hear a jackhammer pounding the asphalt a block away. See the young/old woman call out to Fred to close the window. When he leaves, she fluffs up her pillow and leans back. The jackhammer sounds are softer now. They are coconuts falling as they leave the island.

# Stick

It's a little past three in the afternoon when I find my grandmother on fire in the kitchen. It's just a small section of her sleeve and I pat it out, take the matches from her she used trying to light our electric burner.

At dinner she quietly forks up mashed potatoes my mother is prompting her to eat, the gravy pooled in the crater-like structure Mom's made of them, just like her mother fashioned for her as a kid.

*Mind-weary* is as close as my mother gets to explaining what is happening to Nana. And I say, "Oh." Picture her brain panting like a dog with its tongue hanging out after chasing a stick in the heat like our old dog Freckles, and nothing more is said of it.

Years later, Billy's dad drops dead in the shower and his mom is forced to work at the *Blue Bell Diner*. We take LSD at his house and are playing his dad's old Sinatra records at the wrong speed when Billy says he hears the devil speaking to him with an Italian accent.

"Listen—*there!*" he says.

But I'm too mind-weary at the moment to hear it, busy sniffing the wallpaper roses and hiding all the matches and wondering how a man's heart can explode like a bottle under a truck tire. Just like that. And thinking about Freckles, how all she needed was a stick—back and forth, back and forth—that little pink tongue hanging out and so happy afterwards just to lie down in the shade.

# Transplant

He had a heart pickled in loss and other bitter brines. Its removal was simple—like lake ice cracking. From a sternum to a well they drew from. The Bible, which replaced it, had fly wing-thin white pages.

Nights, when his wife could not sleep, she'd lay her head on his chest, listen to her favorite passages, in lieu of crickets, banging away in the dark.

# The Widow on Fire
## (A Micro-Fable)

*T*he widow was on fire. The neighbors could see her standing by the top floor window of the big house, putting out the curtains she brushed against. At the supermarket she melted all the frozen foods she passed. The checkout clerk was polite, but kept his distance.

The widow on fire met him (a tall, thick man beginning to grey) when the plumbing failed. He was adept at taming water to his bidding, and chewed on the end of a wooden match till it splintered.

The widow on fire would make him stews that painted the walls. The neighbors noted the woman on fire no longer singed the clothes she pinned to the line. But, rather, watched them billow in the sun (a flame too far away to blacken).

In time the widow on fire became, Shirley, and late when the lights were out, she'd stand by the upstairs window and smoke. Her cigarette—its small surrounding light as she inhaled—the only thing that burned.

# Little Heads

All her animals had little heads, disproportionate to the rest of them. There was love in every bite: the canine/feline *gourmet banquets* she dished out. And now these mismatched, too-large bodies were the result

This was her first date in 23 years. Nearly a year since Peter left her, and she wrestled with small talk as though it were an anaconda. He was a supervisor at a Gillette razor blade plant, and she told him, he must be *pretty sharp*. He was watching her rotund tabby jump on a chair (barely) and then onto the table where he licked the plates they had just eaten from. "You don't really need brains to do my job," he said, her rare attempt at wit eluding him.

"Bet you hear that all the time," she went on, hoping it might sink in.

"Hear what?"

"Nothing," she said.

Ben & Jerry, her yellow lab, cozied up and began humping his leg. *"BJ!"* she chided, but the dog would not relent, and the man pushed it away. She noticed he had the tips of two fingers missing. He followed her eyes. "One of the machines," he told her. And that he got a pretty good settlement out of it. "I'm sittin' pretty," he said, putting that same hand on one of her breasts and squeezing it as though he were gauging a beefsteak tomato. "But it still works really good," he told her.

The tabby jumped on the couch beside him, then up his back and onto his head. The man let go and reached up to remove this new hat of pain. *"Fuck!"* he cried out.

"You're gonna get it, mister!" she said, as the cat leapt off (and his hand tunneled through his hair exploring for damage). Not at all sure which of them she was addressing.

# Freeway Jesus

When Joe saw Jesus lying in the middle of the road in his humble robes, he heard a shriek, not unlike that of a castrato or a startled banshee, and realized it was his own.

"*Christ*," Anne said, bracing herself as he veered around a colorfully thorned, blood-speckled head.

"I know," he said. In the last two months he'd run over a cat (mostly black) and more recently, a pigeon (which he didn't think was possible)—and now this.

He looked in his rearview mirror at the huge plaster of paris lawn statue and shook his head. "It's a sign," he said. "And you can believe that."

"And what's it say, Joe?"

"I don't mean a sign, sign. I mean a *sign*. Biblical and shit."

"I get it. And what do you think it means?"

He tossed the joint they were sharing out the window and the unopened bottle of wine they were saving for later.

"*Hey!*"

"That thing was there for a reason."

"Yeah, because some numbnuts didn't tie it down properly and it dropped out the back of his pickup."

"Pretty shallow," he said.

"You're just loaded is all."

"Double pretty shallow," he said. "I don't need the sky to drop down on *my* head." He looked up beyond the clouds. "I get it," he said. "Things are gonna be different. Count on it."

"You mean *more boring than they already are* different?"

"Sure, joke," he said.

But she wasn't. She opened the window, letting the wind whip her hair. What if he'd seen a porta-potty spilled out on the highway, she thought. How might that change things?

She watched him move into the slow lane, stare out at the road intently, bent over the wheel like a little old man. She lit a cigarette and went through a list of possibles in her head. She was young and the list was long.

"Christ," she said.

"Damn straight," he told her. "*I know.*"

# Some Like It Hot

It was my birthday and she was being *Marilyn*. Blonde wig and breathless, popping out of a gown stretched tight. And it was a kick watching her stay in character the whole day. Clicking around in those spiked heels, I knew she hated. Bending over and watering the plants, turning to give me a wink. Not even taking any of it off for a quick one on the couch. Only once yelling at our cat, Roly-Poly, in her real voice for jumping on the table and licking icing off the cake. That steamy Marilyn voice returning quickly, as it leapt off. *You...bad...boy*, said sexy as I ever heard anything spoken. Telling me later, what I needed to pick up from the store: milk (said with a bubbly boil), butter (melting), ice cream (sizzling hot).

# The Incredible Shrinking Woman

Woodchips sprayed from the log as the ax ate into it. The competition was a week away, and this was his strongest event.

From the kitchen she could see him in the yard with his shirt off, warp speed-raining chip mulch against her tea roses. Between the steroids and the fat steaks he bulked up on, she seemed to be shrinking beside him. The way their time together was. And Sandy, their sixteen-year-old, was getting too old to watch *Say Yes to the Dress* with her. Busy being lured to the rocks by that kid with the glued-on jeans who kept showing up in his dad's Caddy.

She took her coffee into the living room and smacked the cup down hard on the table beside the coaster; one of six Ralph had lain out prominently on the walnut burl table he coveted. Clicked on the set. Picked the role of bubble wrap back up and began popping them, one by one. Almost musically. Till they were flat and airless under her thumbs.

# Hawaiian Shirt

The plumber eases out from the cabinet below the sink and asks for a rag. But as Margaret goes through a dusty bag of them in the basement, she is unexpectedly moved.

For there are Frankie's old pajamas: red rockets in a worn-thin outer space. And the yellow dress she wore in Greece—the geometry: *hers*, *its*—so different now. Followed by the ceaseless pull, pull, like a magicians scarf, of Laura's *Sleeping Beauty* bed-sheets—faded with fairies and dreams.

And then she spots it, deep where it was buried—the bright plumerias, still in bloom: his Hawaiian shirt. The one he said made him look "Cheery"—so much younger. Like the Siren, eighteen years his junior, who would draw him to the rocks.

This shirt he wore when he hit her with the news, one hand in his pocket, jingling his keys as they walked. Waiting first for their youngest to leave for college, as though his escape were spring-loaded. The house, too big without them—pinballing through the rooms. Talking to the house plants, the walls—grateful that they didn't talk back.

Margaret pushes all but the shirt back into the bag. These are not fossils, she tells herself. This is not a record of my days. This is a bag of old rags.

It's hot and Margaret undoes the top two buttons of her blouse. "Here you go," she says, stooping to hand the plumber the shirt. He is a man in his forties with a wiry goatee and clear green eyes. Eyes that linger, Margaret notices, in her cleavage as she bends.

"You okay with me using this?" he asks.

"It's just a rag," she tells him. When he takes it, she fans herself. "This heat," she says.

"How about a cold drink?"

"Sure," he says. "I've got some time." He smiles and wipes his hands. Capable hands, she thinks. And as he does, before she heads for the fridge, she watches, with a curious pleasure, the white plumerias blacken.

# A Sky Full of Ghosts

I t's before my first cup of coffee that she declares she's becoming a Buddhist.

"You mean that guy with the fat belly?"

"That's Chinese. I'm thinking Tibetan."

"Wow." There's still crud in my eyes and the cat hasn't been fed yet. It's got a small bell on its collar, and when it wants attention, it scratches like crazy and the little bell jingles. It's jingling.

"I mean, what is heaven anyway, but a sky full of ghosts," she tells me. "Might as well hook up with a religion that believes in second chances. See if I can get it right next time around."

"What if you come back as a flea on a rat's ass?"

"Or a world renown opera singer," she says.

"I thought you hated opera."

"That's not the point. I'd like it *then*."

"What about being on Peaches? Just one of the crowd on Peaches?"

"*What?*"

"A flea on Peaches, dodging all those claws."

"Would you stop it with the flea thing. I'm thinking big. You ought to try it sometime."

"Okay, *Big*," I say, and pour a cup.

She stirs her coffee over and over like she's churning butter. I try to picture her somewhere in Italy singing opera. She's wearing a blonde wig with long braids and is across from this tall chubby guy in a helmet with horns on the sides of it. He's got a beard and they're taking turns singing very loud (in a good way) and the audience loves it. I even see her in her dressing room, later, taking off her make-up. She looks happy. I think to tell her. But figure, it's too late for that.

There's sunlight pouring in and she squints, but doesn't move out of it. We sit across from each other, sipping, staring off and it's very quiet. Except for Peaches' bell, which is pretty damn loud now.

# Interrogating the Dead

I stood over my father's grave, surrounded by angels and bold crosses. Asked him, *Why?* Why *this*, and why *that?* Only the wind answered against the stones. A few crows, like black rags in the branches of a nearby tree, squawked into the fall air.

Across from me, a stately woman in a black dress, shoes, hat, gloves—all that black—bent to place some flowers by a marker. The end of her dress fluttered briefly as I watched, then rose suddenly, exposing a lacy pair of red panties. The incongruity threw me. The woman gathered her dress back slowly with both hands and straightened, moving her lips to where the flowers lay.

When she turned to go, I averted my eyes and returned my gaze to my father's chiseled name. But it was too late. I'd forgotten, completely, where it was I had left off, and the significance of what it was I had come to say.

# In the City of Fog and Mist
## (A Micro-Fable)

*I*t was twilight when we reached the City of Fog and Mist. Sky-scrapers swept past us. A taxi, with a man in a gray fedora sitting in the back, raced toward us. It all dispersed against our trousers. A woman waving from an apartment window sailed off vaporously with her bedroom furniture.

"Sometimes in our travels we must pass through territories such as these—a flowering impermanence," my guide said. Our flashlights pulled us like big dogs on a leash, till we reached the hanging bridge at the edge of the mountain.

My guide took out his knife and banged the handle end hard against a plank. We listened for its reassuring thwack! "It is important to feel certain that there are molecules that know their place in this world, and keep it," he said, as we eased our way across it.

# All the Seasons We Have Never Known

My girlfriend is naked, except for a pair of no-frills panties and furry green slippers, and she is curled over a cello, fused into it, bowing. We'd just made love and then fluttered back to our respective stations. My own, a small table with an old typewriter on it. One that loudly clacks out each letter. Batters the sheet–words, good or bad, declaratively.

It is a music of fits and starts. Greta, across the room, is more reliable. Taken with that deep-throated beast of beauty. She could be playing "Jingle Bells" and it would break your heart.

There is a sloppy metronome outside the window. Bougainvillea thorns scraping against the glass. I take a drink. It warms my belly. Think of all the seasons we have never known. But I am young, and she is young, and the runway is cleared for takeoff.

When I start up again, the clacking is more steady and my fingers and brain connect, pull up bucketsful from a deep well. There is a stray cat we'd taken in that pees on my shoe and a lightbulb that needs to be changed. But our two musics, and everything between, is the only season worth having.

And as I glance over at Greta, who is lost and found in the same moment, I know that this is true.

# About the Author

Robert Scotellaro has published widely in national and international books, journals and anthologies, including W.W. Norton's *Flash Fiction International*, *NANO Fiction*, *Gargoyle*, *New Flash Fiction Review*, *Matter Press*, and many others. Two of his stories were included in *Best Small Fictions* (2016 and 2017). He is the author of seven literary chapbooks, several books for children, and three full-length story collections: *Measuring the Distance*, *What We Know So Far* (winner of The 2015 Blue Light Book Award), and *Bad Motel*. He was the recipient of *Zone 3*'s Rainmaker Award in Poetry. He has, along with James Thomas, edited *New Micro: Exceptionally Short Fiction* published by W.W. Norton & Company (2018). Robert lives with his wife in San Francisco. Visit him at www.rsflashfiction.com.

www.ingramcontent.com/pod-product-compliance
Lightning Source LLC
Chambersburg PA
CBHW032024090426
42741CB00006B/723